ANCIENT ROMAN CLOTHES

Paul Harrison

PowerKiDS
press.

New York

Published in 2010 by The Rosen Publishing Group Inc.
29 East 21st Street, New York, NY 10010

Copyright © 2010 Wayland/The Rosen
Publishing Group, Inc.

First Edition

Series Editor: Julia Adams
Editor: Penny Worms
Series Consultant: Sally Pointer, archaeologist
Designer: Jane Hawkins
Picture Researcher: Kathy Lockley

Library of Congress Cataloging-in-Publication Data

Harrison, Paul, 1969-
  Ancient Roman clothes / Paul Harrison.
    p. cm. -- (Ancient communities: Roman life)
  Includes index.
  ISBN 978-1-61532-304-3 (library binding)
  ISBN 978-1-61532-308-1 (paperback)
  ISBN 978-1-61532-309-8 (6-pack)
  1. Clothing and dress--Rome--Juvenile literature.
  2. Dress accessories--Rome--Juvenile literature.
  3. Beauty, Personal--Rome--Juvenile literature.
  4. Rome--Social life and customs--Juvenile
  literature. I. Title.
  GT555.H37 2010
  391.00937--dc22
                              2009023748

Photographs:
Ancient Art and Architecture Collection: 15T
Ashmolean Museum, University of Oxford, U.K./
The Bridgeman Art Library: 19 Bridgeman Art Library/
Getty Images: 7, 21 Gianni Dagli Orti/Corbis: Titlepage, 22
Mary Evans Picture Library: COVER (main), 9, 10 Mary Evans Picture
Library/Alamy: 6 Heritage-Images: 4, 17 Mimmo Jodice/Corbis: COVER (inset),
18, 28 The London Art Archive/Alamy: 5, 11, 13, 24, 29 Louvre, Paris, France/
Lauros/Giraudon/The Bridgeman Art Library: 12 Araldo de Luca/Corbis:
14 North Wind Picture Archives/Alamy: 20, 27 Photolibrary Group/Photo: Mark
Edward Smith/Tips Italia: 8 Sally Pointer: 23 Private Collection/Archives Charmet/
Bridgeman Art Library: 15B Private Collection/Bridgeman Art Library, London: 26
Steve Sant/Alamy: 16 Nick Turner/Alamy: 25

Manufactured in China

CPSIA Compliance Information: Batch #WAW0102PK: For Further Information

contact Rosen Publishing, New York, New York at 1-800-237-9932

Contents

Words in **bold** can be found
in the glossary.

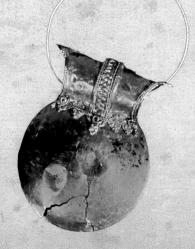

The Roman Empire

The Roman **civilization** grew from a tribe of people into an empire. It lasted for more than 1,000 years, from 753 BCE to 476 CE. At its height, the Roman Empire covered most of Europe and stretched down to northern Africa and into Asia.

ROMAN EMPIRE

The borrowers

The Romans were excellent at borrowing ideas from other countries and civilizations. Once the Romans liked an idea, they improved on it and took it with them across the Empire. Roads were built in countries that had never had roads before. Magnificent buildings were built, and fashions were adopted and spread.

⬆ The Roman Empire stretched across three continents.

Clothing

The Romans were influenced in many ways by older civilizations, such as the **Etruscans** and the Greeks. This included the clothes they wore. However, as the Empire grew, Roman clothing had to change to suit new climates. As they traveled from Italy to hotter or colder places, their traditional Roman clothes were not always comfortable or practical.

 This is a **fresco** of Etruscan musicians. It shows how similar Roman and Etruscan clothing was.

Pliny the Elder (23 CE–79 CE)

Historians know so much about life in the Roman Empire because of writers such as Pliny the Elder. Pliny wrote an encyclopedia called *Natural History*, which recorded much of what the Romans knew about the world, science, and society. Pliny the Elder died during the eruption of Mount Vesuvius, which destroyed the towns of Pompeii and Herculaneum. Pliny died trying to get close to the eruption to write about it.

Menswear

Roman clothing was quite basic, but what a man wore said a lot about the person he was. Just by looking at a man's clothing, you could tell if he was rich or poor, important or a slave.

All-purpose wear

Whether nobleman or slave, every Roman wore a sleeveless item of clothing called a tunic. The tunic was tied with a belt and usually reached down to the knees. It was worn either by itself or covered with a toga (see page 9). During colder months, more than one tunic would be worn at once and a heavy cloak would be worn over the top.

This hunter is wearing a tunic and a cloak.

Togas

The most famous item of Roman clothing is the toga. It was a piece of cloth, shaped like a semicircle, and could be up to 20 feet (six meters) long. The cloth was draped over the left shoulder, wrapped around the body, and then held over the wearer's left arm. The toga was like a badge of honor, since only Roman **citizens** were allowed to wear them. Unfortunately for the Romans, the toga was difficult to wear, because it **restricted** the use of one arm.

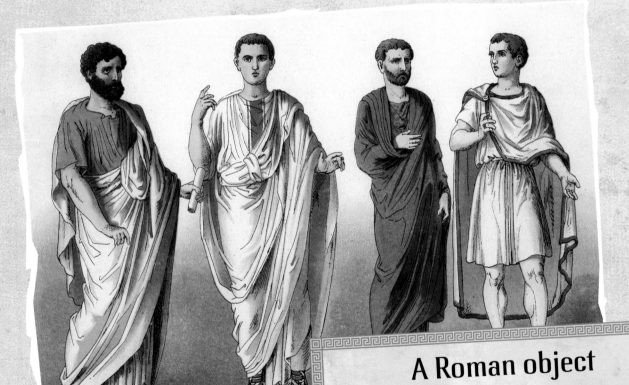

⬆ Togas said a lot about a Roman's place in society. Only the richest people could afford a toga with puple edges, because the dye was very expensive.

A Roman object

Togas came in many different colors and each one was used by a certain type of person or for a special occasion. The usual color was an off-white, but there were also dark-colored ones for mourning. Togas with a purple edge were worn by **magistrates** and **senators**. Purple togas were worn by emperors and by generals during victory parades.

Womenswear

Although women's clothing did not change a great deal throughout the age of the Empire, women had the freedom to wear different styles and colors.

Stola and palla

The everyday item of clothing was a long tunic. It was similar to a man's tunic, only much longer, reaching down to the ground. This *tunica* could have long or short sleeves. If the woman was married, she might choose to wear a sleeveless tunic called a *stola* over the top of the *tunica*. Finally, she would wrap a long, rectangular garment called a *palla* around herself, which she would drape over her hair when going out in public.

⬆ This is a picture from the 1900s showing how Roman women wore their *stolas* and *pallas*.

Underwear

Historians are less sure what the Romans wore under their clothes. It is thought that both women and men wore a kind of **loin cloth** instead of underwear, and women used another strip of cloth as a bra. Rich Roman women also wore what looked like a type of bikini, but it was worn for exercising rather than sunbathing.

This mosaic shows Roman women dancing in bikinis.

Written at the time

Some Romans believed that women should wear plain colors, but not everyone agreed. The Roman historian, Livy, argued that women were not allowed to do many things, so they should at least be allowed colorful clothes:

*"Women cannot partake of **magistracies**, priesthoods, **triumphs**, badges of office, gifts, or spoils of war; elegance, finery, and beautiful clothes are women's badges, in these they find joy and take pride, this our **forebears** called the women's world."*

11

Children's clothes

Roman children were expected to lead adult lives from a young age. Many girls were married by the age of 14. Even the way children dressed looked grown-up, since children wore smaller versions of the clothes that their parents wore.

Junior togas

All Roman boys mostly wore tunics. However, on important occasions boys would have worn a toga. Boy's togas were edged with purple cloth, just like a senator's. Because togas were expensive items of clothing, only boys from rich families could afford one. When the boy reached adulthood, his child's toga would have been replaced with the usual off-white adult toga.

This is a statue of a boy wearing a purple-edged toga. He would have started wearing an adult toga between the ages of 14 and 16.

A Roman object

The *bulla* was a small bag, or locket, that contained a lucky charm. It was worn by Roman children. Both boys and girls wore a *bulla*, which looked like a pouch attached to a necklace. Boys gave up their bullas when they became men, between the ages of 14 and 16; girls stopped wearing theirs when they got married.

⬆ This is a gold *bulla*, which was discovered at Pompeii in Italy.

Doubling up

Both girls and boys wore tunics indoors, but girls would wear a second, longer tunic that reached to the floor when they went out. This tunic would be tied in the middle with a belt, holding up any extra material so it did not drag on the ground and get dirty. This extra piece of material also meant that the tunic could be lengthened as the girl grew.

Textiles

Most Roman clothes were made of wool, though the rich could choose from a wider variety of cloth. Cotton and linen were quite rare, but the most expensive material of all was Chinese silk.

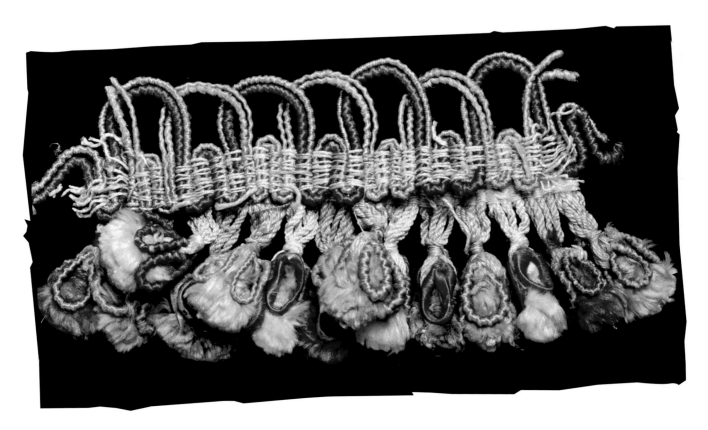

⤒ This is a fringe made of dyed wool. The Romans would use fringes to decorate their clothes.

Wonderful wool

The Romans thought that the best wool came from Belgium and they would carry it back to Rome by ship. Before it could be made into clothes, the wool had to be spun, woven, and dyed the correct color. The Romans mostly used plant dyes, boiling the spun wool or cloth in big vats of color. The most exclusive color was an expensive purple made from shellfish.

A Roman object

The Roman loom was very basic. A large wooden frame was propped upright and strands of wool or cotton yarn were hung from the top. These strands were fastened to weights to keep them stretched tight. Other strands of wool were then woven across and in and out of the vertical strands to make the cloth.

Keeping clean

The Romans had a strange and smelly way of keeping their clothes clean—they washed them in urine! Urine contains **ammonia**, which acts like bleach and was perfect for getting stains out of clothes. The people who had to do the washing were called fullers. It was their job to put the clothes into big barrels of urine, climb in, and move the clothes around using their feet.

Fullers not only washed clothes, as seen here, but they also dyed them.

Footwear

Most people think of Romans wearing sandals, and although this is true, they also had other types of shoe for different occasions. The style of shoe also depended on whether the person wearing them was rich or poor.

Outdoors

Romans wore shoes, not sandals, when walking outdoors, or when they were wearing their togas. These shoes were called *calcei*, and they completely covered the foot. This was much more sensible than wearing sandals outside, because *calcei* offered the feet more protection. *Calcei* were also **status symbols** because slaves were forbidden from wearing them.

A Roman Object

Roman soldiers wore a heavy-duty sandal known as *caligae*. Although they looked flimsy, the sole of the sandal was studded with metal **hobnails**, which gave good grip and a hard surface to kick or stamp on enemies.

Indoors

The famous Roman sandals, or *soleae* as the Romans called them, were considered to be an indoor shoe. Shoes were necessary indoors, because marble floors and mosaics were hard underfoot. If people went visiting another Roman family, they would take their sandals with them to change into when they arrived. Sandals were never worn during meals, since the Romans lay on couches at meal times. Instead, they would be taken off before the meal started and then put back on again when the meal was over.

These two different types of Roman sandal were found in London, England.

Jewelry

During Roman times, men did not wear jewelry apart from a single ring. Women, however, wore a variety of rings, necklaces, **pendants**, earrings, brooches, and hairbands.

Wealth on display

Jewelry was for rich Romans, and nothing said more about a woman's wealth than the jewelry she wore. Most often, Roman jewelry was made from gold, but gemstones and pearls were also very popular. Bracelets and necklaces were often made into the shapes of animals, such as snakes. Both women and men wore rings. Roman rings were made from gold, silver, bronze, or precious stones. Women would sometimes wear rings on every finger. Men were expected to wear only one, simple ring.

Gold necklaces like this one from Pompeii were popular with Romans.

Practical purpose

Not all Roman jewelry was just for display. Clothes did not have buttons or zippers, so were held together with brooches or pins. Poor Romans would have used very simple pins, but rich Romans would have worn highly decorated brooches, **inlaid** with precious gems. Animal shapes were popular for pins, too.

Many pins were made in the shape of animals, such as frogs, lions, and fish.

Written at the time

Pliny the Elder described Roman women's fascination with rings in his work *Natural History*.

"It was the custom at first to wear rings on a single finger only —the one next to the little finger…Later it became usual to put rings on the finger next to the thumb…and more recently still, it has been the fashion to wear them upon the little finger, too. Among the Gauls and Britons, the middle finger—it is said—is used for the purpose. At the present day, however, with us, this is the only finger that is excepted, for all the others are loaded with rings, smaller rings even being separately adapted for the smaller joints of the fingers."

Hairstyles

Roman clothes did not change a great deal over time. However, hairstyles changed often. Both men and women wanted the most fashionable hairstyles, which sometimes meant going to extreme lengths to look good.

Women

During the first century, women's hairstyles consisted of an enormous mass of curls and ringlets, which almost doubled the size of the wearer's head. As Romans came into contact with other nations with different hair colors, hair dyes and wigs also became fashionable. Roman women turned themselves blonde using lime, or they dyed gray hairs with a paste containing lead oxide.

⬇ Some Roman women used headbands to style their hair.

Men

Although men's hairstyles were not as elaborate as women's, Roman men still liked to experiment. At the start of the Roman Empire, men had beards and long hair. Their style gradually changed into a clean-shaven look, with short, straight hair. However, by the time Emperor Hadrian came to power, beards were back in fashion, this time combined with curly, mid-length hair.

This is a bust of the emporer Claudius. During his reign, short hair was very fashionable.

Nero
37 CE—68 CE

Emperor Nero is one of the most **infamous** rulers of the Roman period. He thought of himself as a great writer, singer, musician, and sportsman, but Roman historians tell us that he was none of these things. He certainly had odd ideas about appearance. He would often wear nothing but a beltless dressing gown, and at one point, let his hair grow so long, it went down his back. This was shocking behavior for a Roman.

A Roman makeover

Having the finest clothes, the most expensive jewelry and the most fashionable hairstyle was important to rich Roman women. But they were never completely dressed without their perfume and makeup.

Smelling nice

One of the things that made the Romans so different from other Europeans was their cleanliness. Wealthy Romans bathed every day, which was very unusual at the time. Women wore perfume made from olive oil and sweet-smelling herbs, flowers, and spices, such as cinnamon. Roman houses rarely had bathtubs, so people would go to public bathhouses where they could get washed and talk with friends.

This Roman woman is pouring perfume into a small container called a *vial*.

Dying to look good

The fashionable look for Roman women was pale skin with rosy cheeks, dark eyebrows, and red lips. The way to achieve this look was by using makeup, but this was very different from the makeup of today. The rosy cheeks came from red ocher, a natural mixture of clay and rust. Eyebrows were painted with soot. For pale skin, they covered their faces with a **foundation** that often contained lead. Unfortunately, lead is poisonous and so this makeup could have caused the death of some women.

A Roman object

A Roman makeup box would have looked similar to one today, with foundation, powder, and color for lips and eyes. Roman women would also have to make their own makeup by grinding ingredients such as chalk.

⇩ This is the typical contents of a Roman makeup box.

Perfume bottle

False hair

Hairpin

Foundation

Red ocher

Work clothes

Roman peasants and slaves would have worn simple tunics when going about their work. But even tunics displayed a person's wealth and status—slave's tunics were the shortest and finished above the knee.

In the fields

Wearing tunics was fine in warm countries, but in the colder countries of the Empire, different work clothes were needed. In northern Europe, men who worked outdoors, such as farmers, wore pants and women would wear long woolen stockings. Leather shoes and hooded cloaks helped to keep out the rain and the cold.

These forge workers are wearing short tunics to keep them cool.

Into battle

Some jobs needed special clothing. Soldiers wore either chain mail (a long tunic made of metal rings) or body armor made from strips of metal wired together. Soldiers also wore metal helmets to protect their head, neck, and cheeks. Sometimes they wore metal coverings over their legs and feet. The Romans were always looking at ways of improving their armor. They made many design changes when weaknesses were discovered in battle. For example, helmets had extra strips of metal added to them to offer more protection.

Roman soldiers wore a lot of metal armor to protect them in battle.

Gnaeus Pompeius
106 BCE–48 BCE

Gnaeus Pompeius (who is more often known as Pompey the Great) was the son of a general who rose to be one of the most powerful men in Rome. He was such a successful military leader that he was given three triumphs through Rome. The person whose triumph it was rode in a chariot wearing a purple toga edged with gold **embroidery**, known as the *toga picta*.

Foreign influences

Traditional Roman clothes were based on the clothing worn by the Etruscans and Greeks. As their Empire expanded, the Romans were introduced to different styles and ways of dressing from the countries they conquered.

Keeping warm

The cold and damp weather of northern Europe was very different from the warmer temperatures of Rome. Traditional Roman clothes were not up to the task of keeping the wearer warm or dry, so the Romans borrowed some ideas from the locals—most notably by wearing pants. The northern Europeans also introduced the Romans to a checked pattern, similar to tartan, made by weaving clothes with different-colored threads.

This drawing from the 1800s shows the type of clothing Britons would have worn when the Romans invaded in 55 BCE.

Eastern influence

The far eastern part of the Empire saw some colorful changes to the usual Roman clothes. Although women's clothes could be colorful, they were usually quite plain. In the Far East, clothes began to get more decorative with embroidery, jewels, and pearls sewn into the edges. Even everyday garments, such as tunics, began to look more colorful with embroidered necks and sleeves.

 This illustration from the 1900s shows the highly decorated clothes of the eastern Roman Empire.

Cleopatra VII
69 BCE–30 BCE

Cleopatra VII was the last **pharaoh** of Egypt before it became part of the Roman Empire. She had children with both Roman generals Julius Caesar and Mark Anthony. Rome feared Cleopatra, who was a brilliant **politician**. She joined her army with Mark Anthony's to defeat the Romans, but Egypt was eventually defeated. It became part of the Roman Empire in 30 BCE.

Timeline

BCE

753	Start of the Roman Empire
509	Kings expelled—start of the Roman **Republic**
450	Romans draw up their first set of laws known as the Twelve Tables
387	The Gauls invade and destroy the city of Rome
378	Wall built around the city of Rome
272	Rome takes control of all of Italy
264–241	First Punic War (war with city-state of Carthage)
241	Rome conquers all of Etruscan's lands
218–201	Second Punic War
149	Third Punic War begins
146	Third Punic War ends with Carthage destroyed
66	Asia Minor becomes part of the Empire spreading Roman influence in the east
55	Julius Caesar invades Britain
52	Caesar conquers Gaul
44	Caesar murdered
31	Cleopatra commits suicide and Egypt becomes part of the Empire
27	Augustus becomes emperor. He makes it compulsory for men to wear togas when at senate.

CE

43	Britain finally conquered by the Romans
60–61	Revolt in Britain led by Boudicca
64	Fire destroys much of Rome
79	Vesuvius erupts destroying Pompeii and Herculaneum
80	Colosseum built in Rome
96	Domitian becomes emperor. He makes it compulsory for men to wear togas at the games.
117	Hadrian becomes Emperor and makes beards fashionable again
122	Construction of Hadrian's wall across northern England starts
410	Romans leave Britain
455	The tribe known as the Vandals destroy Rome
476	The end of the Roman Empire

Glossary

Ammonia a natural chemical found in human urine, as well as other sources. It is often used in fertilizer.

Citizens people from Rome who were not slaves. Originally only people from the city of Rome could be citizens, but later, people from all over the empire could call themselves citizens.

Civilizations societies or countries that have laws

Embroidery decorations on cloth made by sewing

Etruscans people from Etruria, a region in northern Italy. Before the Romans, the Etruscans were the greatest civilization in Italy.

Forebears ancestors, the people who lived earlier in history

Frescoes wall paintings which decorated buildings

Gauls a tribe from western Europe. In 387 BCE, the Gauls destroyed the city of Rome. They were a constant problem for the Romans until they were conquered in 52 BCE.

Hobnails nails used in the soles of shoes to protect the bottom of the shoe from wearing out

Infamous having a bad reputation

Inlaid set into. Valuable stones are often inlaid into metal pendants.

Magistracies the authority of the magistrate, a person whose job it is to see that the laws are being followed

Pendant a type of necklace

Politician a person involved with how a country is run

Republic a country run without a king, queen, or emperor in charge

Restricted controlled

Senator a government official. When Rome was a republic, they advised the consuls. During the Roman Empire, they advised the emperors.

Status symbol objects or possessions that show that the owner is wealthy, since only the rich could afford them

Triumphs victory parades held for successful generals or emperors returning from battle

Index

Resources and Web Sites

Ancient Rome! by Avery Hart (Williamson Publishing Company, 2002)

People of the Ancient World: The Ancient Romans by Allison Lassieur (Children's Press, 2005)

Rich and Poor in Ancient Rome by Richard Dargie (Smart Apple Media, 2005)

Web Sites

Due to the changing nature of Internet links, PowerKids Press has developed an online list of Web sites related to the subject of this book. This site is updated regularly. Please use this link to access this list: http://www.powerkidslinks.com/acrl/clothes/